D1567471

LITTLE CRAFT BOOK SERIES

Metal & Wire Sculpture

by elmar gruber

STERLING PUBLISHING CO., INC.,   NEW YORK
IN CANADA: SAUNDERS OF TORONTO LTD.,   DON MILLS, ONTARIO

The Oak Tree Press   LONDON AND SYDNEY

Little Craft Book Series

Candle-Making

Coloring Papers

Creating with Beads

Making Paper Flowers

Metal and Wire Sculpture

Nail Sculpture

Potato Printing

Whittling and Wood Carving

Translated by Gangolf Geis
Photographs by Dr. Richard Sattelmair
Metal figures prepared in collaboration with Georg Blank

Copyright © 1969 by
Sterling Publishing Co., Inc.
419 Park Avenue South, New York 10016.
Simultaneously published and Copyright © 1969 in Canada
by Saunders of Toronto, Ltd., Don Mills, Ontario
British edition published in Great Britain and the Commonwealth by
The Oak Tree Press, Ltd., 116 Baker St., London, W.1.
The original edition was published in Germany under the title
"Arbeiten aus Buntmetall" © 1968 by the Don Bosco Verlag, Munich, Germany.
Manufactured in the United States of America
All rights reserved under the Universal Copyright Convention
and the Berne Convention
Library of Congress Catalog Card No.: 69-19489
Standard Book Number 8069–5128–1
8069–5129–X

Contents

Materials and Tools

Wire and metal sculpture has been growing in interest as an art and craft, with many museums today showing the finest examples of this work. Perhaps at the start you will not be able to create museum pieces, but a thorough study of this book will at least show you the techniques and, hopefully, will give you the inspiration to use your skills and talents to produce work that you will be proud of.

This book shows you by example and by step-by-step instructions how to develop the ability to create objects of beauty and utility from sheet metal and wire. Here, you will deal only with non-ferrous metals—brass and copper—shiny materials.

Here, you will explore the techniques of cutting, bending, perforating and soldering. As you can see from the examples in this book, such simple and elementary handling of the material results in a wide range of forms and structures which can be used for many purposes. The projects illustrated include wall decorations, candle-holders, little baskets, flowerpots, flowers, ash trays, figures, etc. All these things evoke a lot of joy when given as presents: joy for the one who creates them and joy for the one who receives them.

The first materials you need are pieces of sheet metal and some wire, both made of medium-hard copper or brass. The sheet metal should not be thicker than .2 to .4 mm. (36 to 20 gauge). The wire should be from 1.5 to 3 mm. ($\frac{1}{16}$ to $\frac{1}{8}$ inch) in diameter. For some purposes you will also need wire rods made of hardened brass. These materials are obtainable from specialized stores or from larger hobby shops.

All kinds of solder (a fusible metal or alloy), except acid-core, may be used for the soldering of non-ferrous metals. However, if ordinary solid tin solder is used, you have to use it together with a flux (either rosin flux or a mixture of tallow and sal ammoniac). The addition of flux may also be necessary if the chemicals already contained in the core of the self-flux soldering wires are not strong enough to remove the oxide present on the metal. Hardware shops supply solder in wire coils.

Soldering requires an electric soldering iron (100–150 watts) and, if possible, a butane torch. Hobby shops and large department stores often carry soldering sets. In addition to the soldering tools, you have to obtain a heat-resistant base. In many cases a firebrick or a clay brick (clinker brick) may be sufficient; if more difficult works are to be executed it is worthwhile to cover the stone base with an asbestos mat approximately 5mm. ($\frac{3}{16}$-inch) thick.

For cutting sheet metal, use shears made for the purpose (the type used by a jeweler). If you cannot get the "Werindus" sheet metal shears, mentioned in this book, which separates the sheet metal by cutting out an approximate 3-mm. ($\frac{1}{8}$-inch) wide strip, use a double-cut snip, which cuts a $\frac{1}{16}$-inch strip in the metal. Both types of sheet metal

Illus. 1. Few materials and tools are necessary for this craft: an electric soldering iron, a butane soldering torch, pliers, compass, solder wire, jeweler's scissors, brass or copper sheet metal, and an asbestos mat to work on.

shears may be obtained from specialized shops. A simple scissors will also do in case nothing else is obtainable. The wires can be cut effortlessly with pincers or multiple-purpose pliers.

Bending the cut metal into desired shapes sometimes requires the aid of a tool such as flat-nose pliers, pointed pliers or multiple-purpose pliers. A little vise used as a holding device can often be very helpful. A chisel and hammer will also be useful.

Perforating the sheet metal is done with the aid of a nail or other puncturing tool, such as an iron rod or a chisel, and a hammer. Before doing this, the workpiece is placed on a yielding base (wooden board).

Methods

THE BENDING OF WIRE

For many works you will need a large number of wire pieces bent into the same shape. You obtain these construction elements by bending soft brass or copper wire over a form. Hammer wire nails into a piece of wood in a pre-designed pattern. Then bend the wire around the nails so that it takes the desired form. (See Diagram 1.)

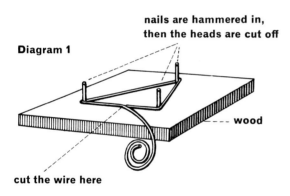

Diagram 1

nails are hammered in, then the heads are cut off

wood

cut the wire here

The nails have to be strong and hammered deeply into the wood in order to withstand the pressure created by bending the wire. Pinch the nailheads off with nippers or cutting pliers so that the finished piece of wire can be lifted off easily. When the end of the wire reaches the starting point, you cut it. The two ends that touch are soldered together. In this way you can duplicate a form as many times as you wish.

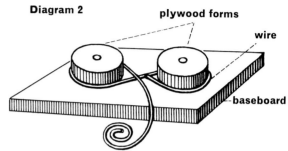

Diagram 2   plywood forms

wire

baseboard

In dealing with more complicated forms, it is advisable to use plywood shapes instead of nails. Take pieces of plywood sawed out according to the desired figure and fix them on to a baseboard (use all-purpose glue and small nails). Then bend the wire around the plywood contours (See Diagram 2). Proceed with cutting and soldering each wire shape as you did when forming the element around nails.

Wire rings of uniform size can be made by

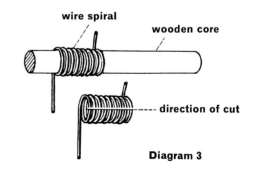

wire spiral

wooden core

direction of cut

Diagram 3

winding the wire around a piece of round wood (dowel). The wire spiral is then slipped off the wooden core and cut open longitudinally with nippers or cutting pliers (See Diagram 3). Then the two ends of each wire ring thus obtained are soldered together. Wire may also be wound around a bar of wood in the same fashion, resulting in squares or rectangles.

TREATMENT OF SHEET METAL SURFACE

The even surface of sheet metal can be varied according to your taste in simple ways without the application of embossing or engraving techniques.

The sheet metal can be decorated by incisions made with a chisel and hammer or with a pair of scissors. The "Werindus" sheet metal shears cuts out of the sheet metal a 3-mm. wide strip which rolls itself up. Thus at the end of each incision there remains a curl which sometimes has a very decorative effect. (See Illus. 27.)

Another possibility is provided by the use of a punch and a hammer. You can knock out small discs from the sheet metal—either wholly or, by holding the punch inclined, partly so that the discs

Illus. 2. The candleholder (cylinder within which you place a candle) was perforated and incised so the light would shine through. For the bracelet, copper wire was soldered on to a piece of curved brass.

still remain connected at one spot to the whole piece, from which they can be bent up.

To perforate the sheet metal, place it on a wooden board; now, with the aid of a hammer and punching tool (a nail, chisel, squared iron, etc., according to the desired form and size) simply punch the holes through. The jagged edges give a decorative (scraper-like) effect. The arrangement of the perforated holes and the choice of the size of the holes permits unlimited possibilities. (See Illus. 25 and 39.)

Solder, too, may be used for ornamentation. The soldering flame has to be handled very carefully in order to prevent the solder—as a result of excess heat—from simply flowing out flatly without forming a shape. (See Illus. 51.) In addition, pieces of wire to be soldered on the metal surface can be bent and arranged in order to create an ornamental effect. (See Illus. 2, previous page.)

Any or all of these treatments may certainly be combined.

SOLDERING

The soldering process is very simple. The spots or areas to be joined are first heated with the soldering iron or with the butane torch. Then, if necessary, flux is applied and the metal is heated until the melting temperature of the solder is reached.

Now the solder itself is applied by melting it with the tip of the iron until it flows on to the joint. In the case of the electric soldering iron, best results are obtained by touching the joint with the hot iron at the same time as you are melting the solder.

The oxide that accumulates at the tip of the soldering iron has to be removed frequently. File it off and "re-tin" the tip by dipping it in rosin and then coating it with solder. Failures in soldering result mostly from the fact that the parts to be joined are not hot enough; this prevents the solder from fusing properly.

The soldering torch has one advantage over the soldering iron: it heats the junction to be soldered much faster and over a wider area and thus spreads the flux and solder to form a very good fusion. However, you must take care not to burn the metal. Overheating results in a change of color. However, this may sometimes be an advantage. Experiment and find out.

Soldering of Flat Works

In soldering flat works you do not need a holding device for the parts to be joined. You arrange the pieces of wire or sheet metal on the heat-resistant base according to your design. Heat the joints (best done with the soldering torch) and let the solder melt. As non-ferrous metals are very good heat conductors, you have to take care that the solder does not melt too far and does not cover up space you do not want to be covered.

Illus. 3. Materials and tools needed for soldering metal and wire: soft brass wire, wire cutters, pliers, butane torch, self-flux soldering wire, soldering iron, an asbestos mat, and sheets of metal (see page 5).

Illus. 4. In this flat work, rectangular pieces of copper and brass sheeting are soldered together by heating the areas to be joined with a butane soldering torch and letting the solder wire melt on to each joint. An asbestos work mat is used.

Soldering of Construction Works

In doing this type of work you build from the base upwards. Take, for instance, a little basket: The bottom is first executed as a flat work and then element after element is soldered on to it in an upward direction. This "upward soldering" can only be done with the soldering iron, as a soldering torch would melt the already existing connections.

After starting such a work, you will soon realize that your hands are not sufficient. You will need an assistant. The helper holds the parts together so that you are able to execute the actual soldering with the soldering iron and the soldering wire. The helper should either wear old leather gloves, or hold the parts with insulated pliers to avoid being burned.

Instead of using a helper, you can fashion a holding device by pushing the metal into the asbestos base, by jamming it between pieces of brick, or by the use of a vise. Flat works and construction works may also be combined.

After soldering is complete, the work will need further treatment. If flux (as rosin flux or tallow and sal ammoniac) has been used, the greasy

Illus. 5. Wrap the brass wire in a tight spiral around a wooden dowel. Then cut the spiral along its length, making rings.

residue has to be washed off the completed workpiece with a hot alkaline solution. (Use a brush.) For the preservation of the brightness of nonferrous metals a coating of cellulose lacquer, obtainable from paint shops, is recommended.

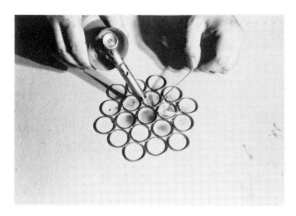

Illus. 6. Using the asbestos mat to work on, heat the rings and the solder with the torch until the solder melts and flows on to the parts you want to join. The rings will become the bottom of a basket.

Illus. 7. In order to solder the rings in a vertical position, you will need a helper to hold the rings upright for you with pliers. Use a soldering iron not a torch so as not to melt the already soldered joints.

Illus. 9. Row after row is added to the basket. Here the helper uses a leather work glove to protect his hand from the heat as he holds the brass ring. The finished work is similar to the one in Illus. 28.

Illus. 8. Two rings are attached in an upright position.

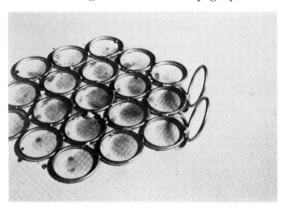

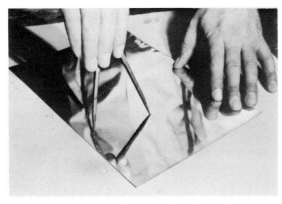

Illus. 10. To make a brass bowl such as the one in Illus. 32, first outline a circle on the metal sheet with the compass.

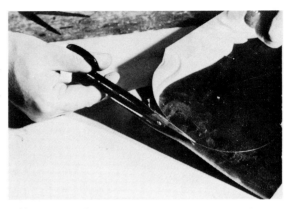

Illus. 11. With the jeweler's scissors, cut the circle out.

Illus. 12. From the circle, cut out a section about one-quarter the size of the circle. This section will be used later as part of the bowl's base.

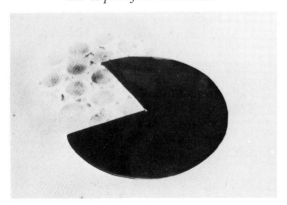

Illus. 13. Bend the metal circle into a cone shape, over-lapping the edges where the quarter-section was cut out.

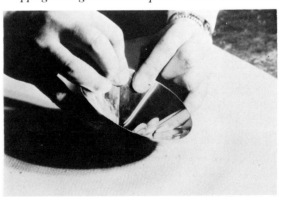

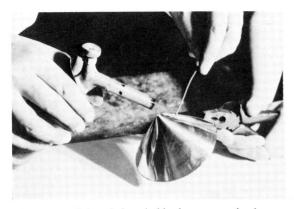

Illus. 14. While a helper holds the cone with pliers, you solder the overlapping edges together with a butane torch.

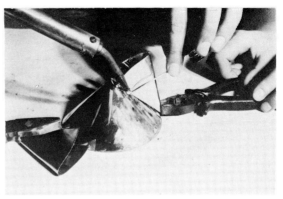

Illus. 15. Cut two more quarter circles the same size as the first section you cut out of the metal circle. Bend each section in the middle and solder each on to the bottom of the cone as shown. Use a soldering iron.

Illus. 16. The electric soldering iron is used rather than the butane torch so that the soldered seam of the cone is not melted or weakened.

Illus. 17. The bowl will be useful as an ash tray or as a candy dish.

13

Flat Works

Illus. 18. Wire pieces of varying widths and some pieces of brass tubing were soldered into rectangular shapes.

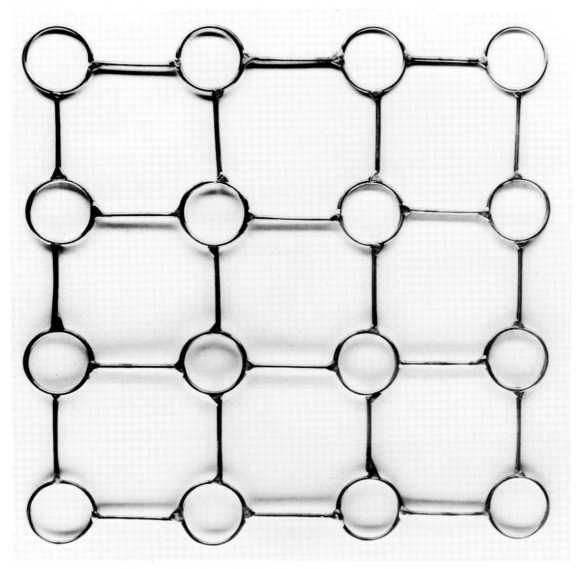

Illus. 19. Wire rings and wire pieces of the same size form this pattern.

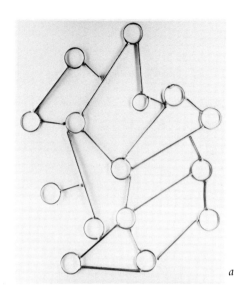

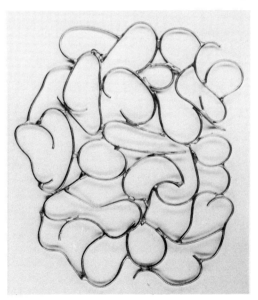

Illus. 20. Wire designs: (a) This design consists of wire rings and pieces of straight wire of varying lengths. (b) An amorphous shape was made of bent wire of varying lengths. (c) Here is a spider web made of wire spokes and slightly bent wire pieces.

c

a

b

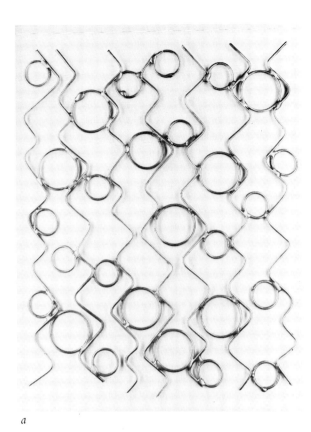

a

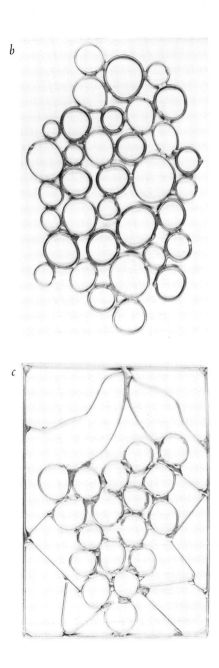

b

c

Illus. 21. Characteristic of these three examples is the use of wire rings of varying sizes: (a) waves and bubbles; (b) soap bubbles; (c) grapes.

17

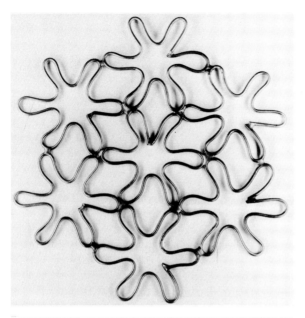

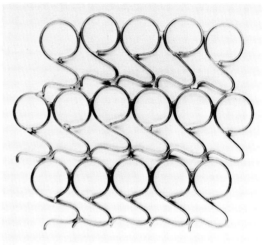

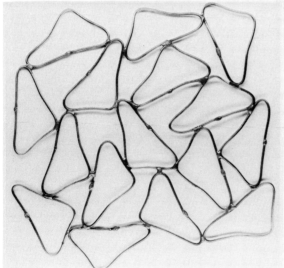

Illus. 22. These three examples show how the same wire form can be used repeatedly. The bending of different pieces of wire into the same shape is described on page 6.

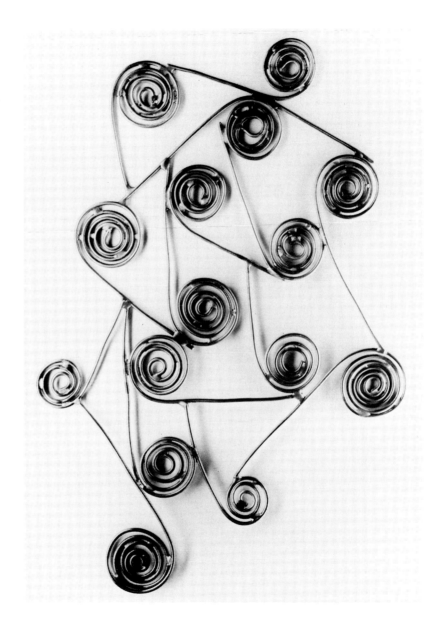

Illus. 23. The elements of this work were bent without a mould. Each wire was bent into a spiral with the aid of a pair of pliers.

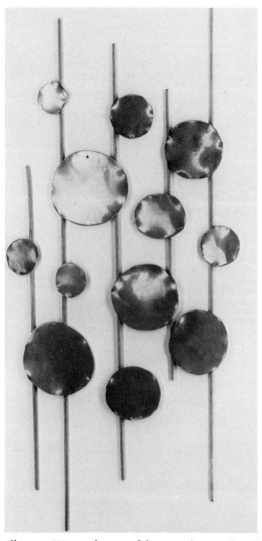

Illus. 24. Wire and pieces of sheet metal are combined.

Illus. 25. Here three amorphous pieces of metal are soldered on wire rods. The middle of the metal pieces are perforated.

Illus. 26. Copper and brass pieces cut from sheet metal are alternated in this soldered design. The change in color, resulting from the soldering torch, was retained.

Illus. 27. The holes were knocked out with a hammer and punch; the strips, rolled up automatically, were cut out with "Werindus" sheet metal shears.

Construction Works

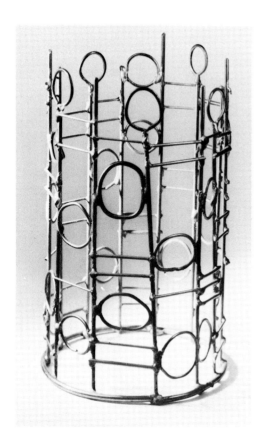

Illus. 28. These upright objects made of wire rings and wire rods are used as candle sleeves or holders. They were made with the use of a soldering iron.

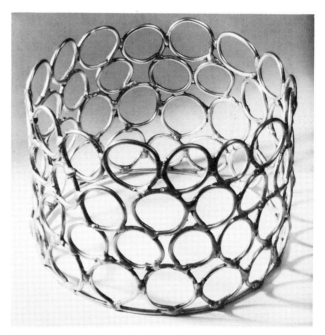

Illus. 29. The holder of the white candle was soldered as a flat work and then rolled up. To hold the dark candle you must solder a flat base within the cylinder.

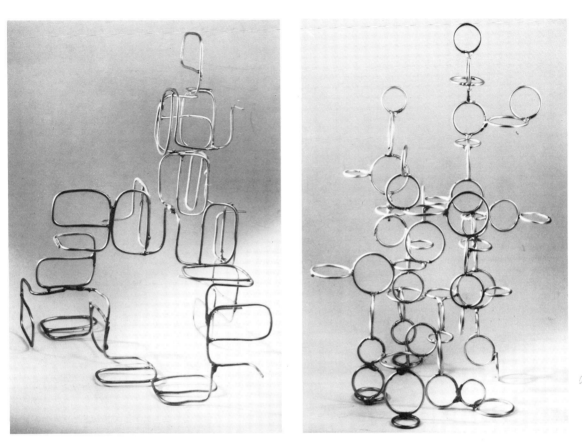

Illus. 30. These abstract figures are made of repeated wire shapes soldered in an upright manner. The shaping of the wire to produce the same form again and again is described on page 6.

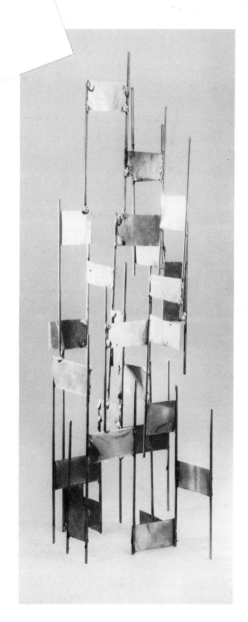

Illus. 31. Upright abstract figures can also be made of pieces of metal alone (below), or metal pieces combined with wire rods (left).

Illus. 32. How to make a cone-shaped candy bowl or ash tray is described at the beginning of the book.

Illus. 33. The separate, rectangular pieces of this brass cachepot (planter) are soldered together and ornamented by copper pieces soldered on.

Sheet Metal and Stones

On excursions and walking tours, you can often discover the "preciousness" of very ordinary stones. Streaks of iron and minerals, etc., give many a stone color and brightness. These stones can be used for wall decorations by mounting them on brass or copper sheet metal.

The form of the sheet-metal base must be shaped in a way that leads the eye towards the stone. The stone should not appear as a mere decoration on the sheet metal; it should be the focal point.

The stone is held either by unobtrusive pieces of sheet metal soldered on to the base or by sheet metal parts which are soldered on consciously as part of the design.

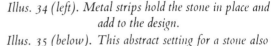

Illus. 34 (left). Metal strips hold the stone in place and add to the design.

Illus. 35 (below). This abstract setting for a stone also uses simple, metal strips.

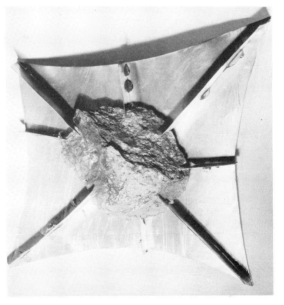

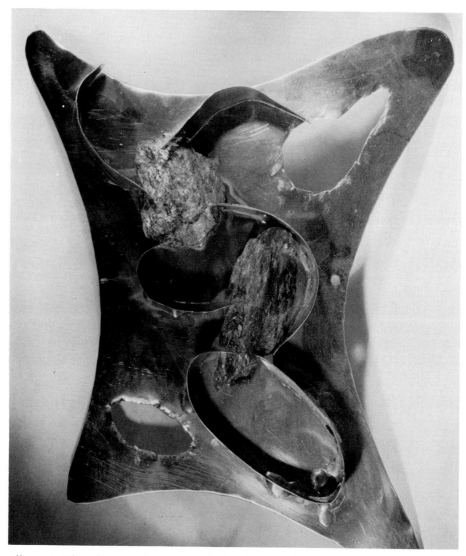

Illus. 36. This abstract rock setting is further decorated by abstract holes cut out with a hammer and chisel.

Flowers

Simple flower heads are obtained by cutting metal discs to the desired form using the radii as a guide. (See Diagram 1.) The flower petals are shaped and bent up according to one's own desire. The longitudinal ribs in the petals can be achieved with a hammer and a chisel, using a wooden base and hammering just enough to indent the metal, not cut it. The bottom of the blossom can be created by perforating the metal sheet with a nail. Bore a hole for the stem.

Rosette-like flower heads combine three to five bloom-discs of different diameters, each created in the way just described. Hold the stem in a vise. Put the bloom-discs on the stem one on top of the other so that the smallest disc appears as the core of the flower head (See Diagram 2). Solder each disc to the stem immediately after the lining-up. (Rods of hard brass are most suitable for the stems.)

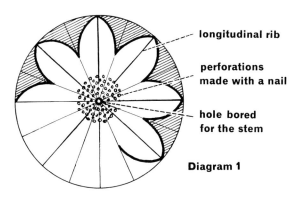

longitudinal rib

perforations
made with a nail

hole bored
for the stem

Diagram 1

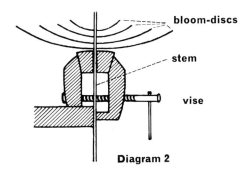

bloom-discs

stem

vise

Diagram 2

31

Illus. 37. The parallel leaves were cut out as one piece. A hole was made in the middle, and the rod used for the stem was pushed through and soldered on.

Illus. 38. The metal strips (of copper foil) were cut out with ordinary scissors.

33

Illus. 39. The middle of these sunflowers get their grated texture through the perforation process.

Illus. 40. For each tulip, three pairs of petals were cut. The petals opposite each other were cut symmetrically out of one piece of metal.

Illus. 41. The petals of this imaginative flower were shaped into the ray design by using a hammer and a wide, flat chisel.

Illus. 42. The stamens are made of thin wire. Small pieces of solder are added to the end.

Illus. 43. The stems of these roses are inserted into small holes drilled in the Plexiglas base.

Illus. 44. Making these flowers requires a great deal of patience and sensitivity to achieve the decorative effect of such intricate work.

Figures of Sheet Metal

Pieces of sheet metal are transformed by cutting and bending them until they have taken on a form sufficient to the imagination or fantasy. Full plastic figures can be created by piecing together various parts and soldering together the cut edges. This technique can lead to very artistic results.

Illus. 45. Simple soldered forms are shown by a pyramid and a cube.

Illus. 46. The arms, legs and trunk of this figure were cut out in one piece. The neck, face, nose and forehead were cut out as separate, single pieces, then were bent and soldered.

Illus. 47. For this imaginative fruit, the different parts were cut out in segments—like the segments of a ball—and soldered together into their round shape.

Illus. 48. The figure on the right was made of three pieces of shaped metal soldered together. The figure on the left has more pieces, but the process is the same.

Illus. 49. With this penguin, and the rooster on the cover, the various techniques of working with metal and wire are used to produce a complete sculpture.

A Play with Light

The illustrated lamp is meant to be an inspiration for the use of the mirror-effect of the blank metal. The individual "sails" are soldered as flat works and are then arranged in a semicircle in the holes of the baseboard so that the sheet parts (the sails soldered on to wire rods) are interlocked.

The flame of the candle itself ought to be covered by the sails; only its rays ought to come into play through reflections on the metal. By turning the sails, different effects are obtained.

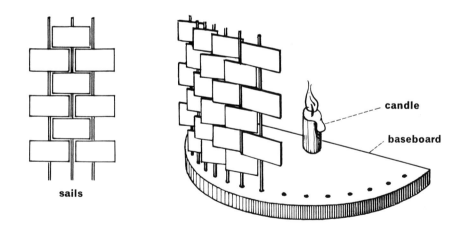

sails

candle

baseboard

45

Illus. 50. The metal sails cover the candle but reflect its rays.

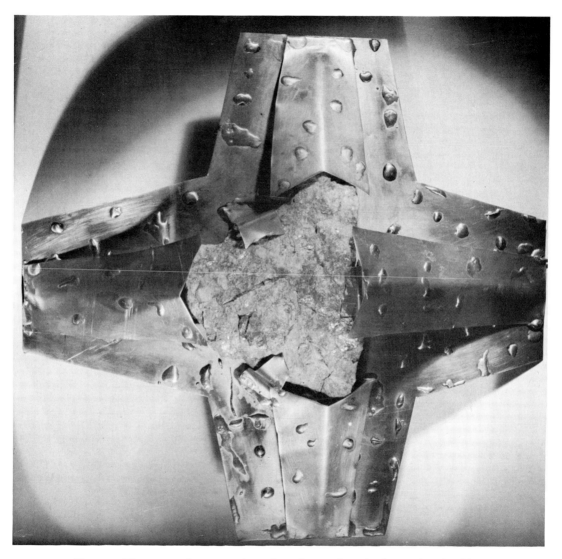

Illus. 51. This setting for a stone shows how the metal can be decorated with solder.

Index